The Accidental Zucchini

AN UNEXPECTED ALPHABET

Max Grover

Browndeer Press
Harcourt Brace & Company
SAN DIEGO   NEW YORK   LONDON

Requests for permission to make copies
of any part of the work should be mailed to:
Permissions Department,
Harcourt Brace & Company
8th Floor, Orlando, Florida 32887.

Library of Congress Cataloging-in-Publication
Data available upon request.
ISBN 0-15-276716-9

First edition
ABCDE

The paintings in this book were done in acrylics
on D'Arches Lavis Fidelis drawing paper.
The display and text type was set in
Belucian by Harcourt Brace & Company
Photocomposition Center, San Diego, California.
Color separations by Bright Arts, Ltd., Singapore
Printed and bound by Tien Wah Press, Singapore
Production supervision by Warren Wallerstein and Ginger Boyer
Designed by Michael Farmer

To all those who have helped and shown
—Max

Apple autos

Bathtub boat

Cupcake canyon

Dog dance

Elephant elevator

Fork fence

Goldfish grandstand

Hotel hop

Ice-cream island

Junk jungle

Kite kazoos

Letter ladders

Macaroni merry-go-round

Neon night

Octopus overalls

Peach pie pile

Quilt queen

Railroad race

Sailor salad

Tuba truck

Umbrella underwear

Vegetable volcano

Whistle washers

extra X's

Yawn yard

Zigzag zoo